OUTDOOR EXPLORERS
3 Midwest

Helen Foster James

Published in the United States of America
by Cherry Lake Publishing
Ann Arbor, Michigan
www.cherrylakepublishing.com

Reading Adviser: Marla Conn MS, Ed., Literacy specialist, Read-Ability, Inc.

Photo Credits: ©Tatiana Bobkova / Shutterstock.com, cover, 1; © ESB Professional / Shutterstock.com, 6; © Mayabuns / Shutterstock.com, 8, 13; ©Laura Fieldhouse / Shutterstock.com, 10; ©Colin D. Young / Shutterstock.com, 10; © Steve Shoup / Shutterstock.com, 11; ©Sadovskaia Irina / Shutterstock.com, 11; © Artulina / Shutterstock.com, 12; © PAKULA PIOTR / Shutterstock.com, 12; © Edgar Lee Espe / Shutterstock.com, 13; © Kat Grant Photographer / Shutterstock.com, 14, 18; © Geoffrey Kuchera / Shutterstock.com, 16; ©RRuntsch / Shutterstock.com, 16; © Brad Thompson / Shutterstock.com, 17; ©Joe Lamastra / Shutterstock.com, 17; © suebmtl / Shutterstock.com, 18; © ecliptic blue / Shutterstock.com, 19; © BGSmith / Shutterstock.com, 19; © FamVeld / Shutterstock.com, 20; © stefanolunardi / Shutterstock.com, 20; © STUDIO JH / Shutterstock.com, 20; © urbans / Shutterstock.com, 20; © dmodlin01 / Shutterstock.com, 22; © Hank Erdmann / Shutterstock.com, 22; ©Jon Manjeot / Shutterstock.com, 22; © Zack Frank / Shutterstock.com, 22

Library of Congress Cataloging-in-Publication Data
Names: James, Helen Foster, 1951- author.
Title: Midwest / Helen Foster James.
Description: Ann Arbor : Cherry Lake Publishing, 2017. | Series: Outdoor explorers | Includes bibliographical references and index. | Audience: Grades K to 3.
Identifiers: LCCN 2016057043| ISBN 9781634728768 (hardcover) | ISBN 9781634729659 (pdf) | ISBN 9781534100541 (pbk.) | ISBN 9781534101432 (hosted ebook)
Subjects: LCSH: Natural history—Middle West—Juvenile literature.
Classification: LCC QH104.5.M47 J36 2017 | DDC 508.77—dc23
LC record available at https://lccn.loc.gov/2016057043

Cherry Lake Publishing would like to acknowledge the work of the Partnership for 21st Century Skills. Please visit www.p21.org for more information.

Printed in the United States of America
Corporate Graphics

Table of Contents

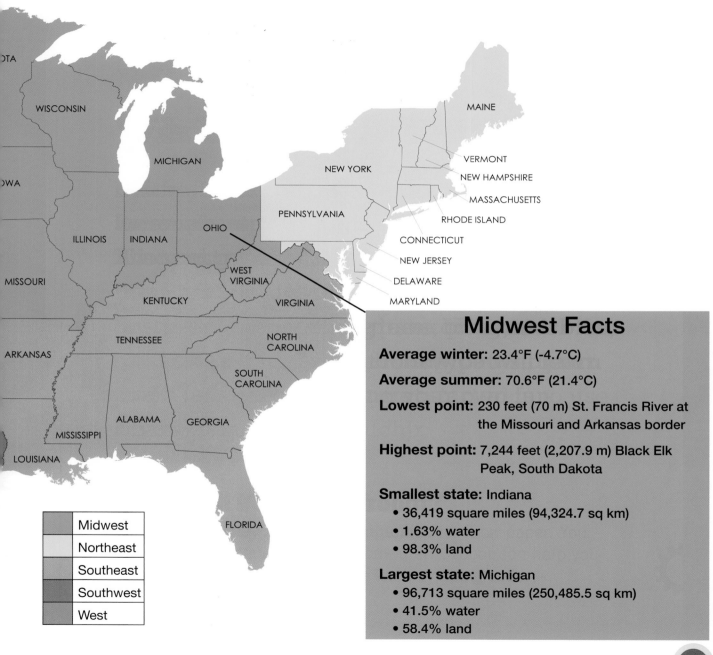

Midwest Facts

Average winter: 23.4°F (-4.7°C)

Average summer: 70.6°F (21.4°C)

Lowest point: 230 feet (70 m) St. Francis River at the Missouri and Arkansas border

Highest point: 7,244 feet (2,207.9 m) Black Elk Peak, South Dakota

Smallest state: Indiana
- 36,419 square miles (94,324.7 sq km)
- 1.63% water
- 98.3% land

Largest state: Michigan
- 96,713 square miles (250,485.5 sq km)
- 41.5% water
- 58.4% land

	Midwest
	Northeast
	Southeast
	Southwest
	West

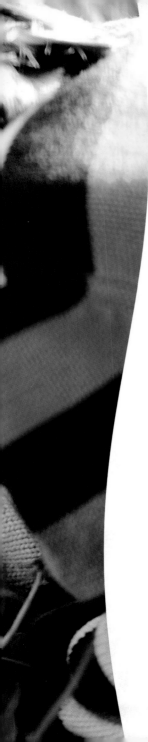

It's time for a nature hike. Let's see what we can see.

? Indiana's official state flower is the peony.
Why do you think this is?

Plants

I notice all the pink, purple, and yellow flowers. Their buds are all in **bloom**. I see a bee resting on a peony!

Different trees line the sidewalk. Some trees have flowers. Other trees have nuts.

American Elm Tree

- North Dakota's official state tree since 1947.

- The inside bark can be made into rope.

Dwarf Lake Iris

- Michigan's official state wildflower since 1998.

- This uncommon flower is found only by the Great Lakes.

Eastern Cottonwood Tree

- Official state tree of Kansas and Nebraska.

- It is one of the fastest growing trees in the United States.

Goldenrod

- Nebraska's official state flower since 1895.

- The entire plant can be used as medicine.

Oak Tree

- The United States' official national tree since 2004.

- Most oak trees don't lose their leaves during fall and winter.

Ohio Buckeye Tree

- Ohio's official state tree since 1953.

- The nut that grows on the tree looks like the eye of a buck, or a male deer.

Peony

- Ants are attracted to the **nectar** the peonies make.

- The blooms can get as large as 10 inches (25 centimeters).

Showy Lady's Slipper

- Minnesota's official state flower since 1967.

- During its first year, it might grow only as tall as a new pencil.

The northern cardinal is the official state bird of Illinois, Indiana, Kentucky, North Carolina, Ohio, Virginia, and West Virginia. Which of these states are in the Midwest?

Animals

I hear the song of a meadowlark. I hear a robin singing, too. A red bird is looking at me. It's a cardinal.

I see a furry animal digging a hole. It has a white stripe down its face.

American Badger

- Wisconsin's official state animal since 1957.

- They use their sharp claws to dig burrows underground.

American Robin

- Official state bird of Michigan and Wisconsin.

- The male and female take turns feeding their young.

Common Loon

- Minnesota's official state bird since 1961.

- They spend most of their time swimming in lakes and ponds.

Coyote

- South Dakota's official state animal since 1949.

- These animals can walk on the tips of their toes.

Eastern Goldfinch

- Iowa's official state bird since 1933.

- Females lay pale blue eggs in waterproof nests.

Northern Cardinal

- Males are bright red and females are pale brown.

- Both male and female cardinals sing.

Ornate Box Turtle

- Kansas' official state reptile since 1986.

- The turtle protects itself from predators by hiding in its shell.

Western Meadowlark

- Official state bird of Kansas, Nebraska, and North Dakota.

- Females build their nests on the ground in grassy areas, like prairies.

Spring

Summer

Fall

Winter

Weather

During spring, I find small flowers peeking through the melting snow.

The summer sun is hot. It's windy. The wind blows the trees and the grass.

The fall air is cool. I walk through a pile of red and orange leaves. I like the crunching sound they make.

Sometimes it snows during winter. Sometimes it rains. The water becomes ice. I try not to fall.

Lake

Prairie

Farmland

Bluff

Geography

Some lakes are small. Other lakes look as big as the ocean.

There are wildflowers and grass growing in the prairie. Where did all the trees go?

I see large rolls of hay in a field. What type of farm is this?

I notice hills that look like small mountains.

Where would you like to hike?

Find Out More

Fleming, Denise. *In the Small, Small Pond*. New York: Henry Holt, 1993.

Fleming, Denise. *In the Tall, Tall Grass*. New York: Henry Holt, 1991.

Glossary

bark (BAHRK) the tough covering on the stems of shrubs, trees, and other plants
bloom (BLOOM) the flowering state; flower
burrows (BUR-ohs) tunnels or holes in the ground made or used as homes by animals
Great Lakes (GRAYT LAYKS) a group of five freshwater lakes between the United States and Canada; the Great Lakes are made up of Lake Superior, Lake Huron, Lake Ontario, Lake Michigan, and Lake Eerie
medicine (MED-ih-sin) helpful drugs used to treat illnesses
nectar (NEK-tur) a sweet liquid from flowers
prairies (PRAIR-ees) large areas of flat or rolling grassland with few or no trees
predators (PRED-uh-tors) animals that live by hunting other animals for food
protects (pru-TEKTS) keeps something safe from harm, attack, or injury
reptile (REP-tile) a cold-blooded animal with scaly, dry skin that crawls across the ground or creeps on short legs

Index

About the Author

Helen Foster James is a volunteer interpretive naturalist for her local state park. She lives by the ocean and loves to hike in the mountains. She is the author of *S Is for S'mores: A Camping Alphabet* and more than 20 other books for children.